To my boys, for their inspiration.

Happy Day Out on the Sunshine Coast
Finn & Henry explore!

Author – Megan Carige
Illustrator – Honey Randall

Happy Day Out on the Sunshine Coast
Author – Megan Carige

© Megan Carige 2018

First published 2018
Second edition 2020

www.happydayout.com.au
happydayoutbook@gmail.com

This book is sold with the understanding that the author is not offering specific personal advice to the reader. Although the author and illustrator have tried to make the information as accurate as possible, they accept no responsibility for any loss or risk, personal or otherwise, that happens as a consequence of the use and application of any of the contents of this book.

All rights reserved. This book may not be reproduced in whole or part, stored, posted on the internet, or transmitted in any form or by any means, electronic, mechanical, photocopying, recording, or other, except brief extracts for the purpose of review, without written permission from the author of this book.

Editing and publishing by: Alex Fullerton www.authorsupportservices.com
Illustrated by: Honey Randall

ISBN: 978-0-9876158-5-5

A catalogue record for this book is available from the National Library of Australia

Let's have a happy day together!

We have a happy time playing on the beach. We build sandcastles and play with our diggers. The sand CRUNCHES under our feet when we walk.

Crunch-crunch-cccrruunch

We are happy riding our bikes
along the esplanade.
Look at the ocean,
what a view!

We have a happy time fishing off the jetty.
WAITING...WAITING...WAITING
to catch a fish!

We are happy eating ice cream at Bulcock Beach. YUMMY!

We have a happy time kayaking at Golden Beach. We hear the squelching water underneath us. The water is so blue. There is a pelican too!

We are happy when we visit a farm in Maleny. We help feed the cows.

Moooooo

We have a happy time playing in the water fountain at Kings Beach.

We are happy when we go on the boat.
Boating is fun and there is
lots to see out on the

We have a happy time hiking up
Mt Beerburrum. It is really high up there.
We can see all the Glass House Mountains.

We are happy at Sea Life Sunshine Coast Aquarium in Mooloolaba. We get to see what lives under the ocean!

We have a happy time walking through the Noosa National Park.

LOOk, there's a koala!

We are happy at the rock pools at Shelly Beach. We look for crabs, shells, fish and other sea creatures. Oh look, there's a whale going past!

We are happy but tired when we spot the big ships going past the coastline of Caloundra. They are so amazing lit up at night!

We hope you had a happy day with us.

Turn the page to follow in Finn
& Henry's footsteps....

Tick off the sites you visited with Finn & Henry...

- [ ] Play on the beach
- [ ] Ride bikes
- [ ] Go fishing
- [ ] Visit Bulcock Beach
- [ ] Go kayaking
- [ ] Visit a farm and feed the cows
- [ ] Play in the water fountain at Kings Beach

- [ ] Go for a boat ride
- [ ] Hike up Mt Beerburrum
- [ ] Visit Sea Life
- [ ] Visit the Noosa National Park
- [ ] Visit the rock pools at Shelly Beach
- [ ] Spot the ships at night

About the Author

MEGAN CARIGE spent her earlier childhood living in Fiji before her family moved to Toowoomba. Megan has spent most of her adult life living, working and visiting cities around Australia and the world.

Recently moving back to live in the beautiful Garden City of Toowoomba with her two young sons, gave Megan the inspiration for her first children's story book, *Happy Day Out in Toowoomba*.

Megan's second book, *Happy Day Out on the Sunshine Coast* is now part of the successful *Happy Day Out* book series. You can see more by visiting: www.happydayout.com.au.

About the Illustrator

HONEY RANDALL is a Queensland girl through and through, and has lived in several locations around the Sunshine State.

She enjoys drawing and writing, and works mostly digitally with the occasional piece using traditional pencils and pens.

Happy day out on the Sunshine Coast is Honey's first children's book and she plans on becoming a full time illustrator.

Find more of her work on Instagram: honey_elizabeth_illustration

www.ingramcontent.com/pod-product-compliance
Lightning Source LLC
Chambersburg PA
CBHW040210020526
44112CB00041B/2930